Jared Romey & Diana Caballero

BABY NAMES FROM PUERTO RICO

Trendy, Creative and Unique Names from the Island of Enchantment

LANGUAGE BABEL, INC.

For ordering information or special discounts for bulk purchases, please contact
Language Babel, Inc. 1357 Ashford Ave., PMB 384, San Juan, PR 00907 or by
e-mail to info@speakinglatino.com.

Jared Romey also publishes a blog and materials for other Spanish speaking
countries. For more information about Speaking Latino, visit our web site at
www.SpeakingLatino.com.

Facebook Pages
Speaking Latino
Jared Romey

Twitter
@jaredromey

Google +
Speaking Latino

TABLE OF CONTENTS

INTRODUCTION

If you visit the Island of Enchantment, you may notice that many of the young people's names are unknown to you. Apparently the tradition of naming the children to preserve the memory of mom or dad is not used anymore.

Puerto Ricans are very creative and unique in this process of naming their children. Today, for us is not enough to name our baby with a simple common name in Spanish such as María, Ana, Pedro, Antonio o Luis. Now, the trend is to create new, unique names for our babies. This creative process often occurs when we combine names, for example the names of both parents or two names we like. That is why it is common to have friends with names such as Kathyenid (woman), Jonathaniel (man), Kaoru (woman) or Sadiel (man).

Baby Names Around the World

Some countries regulate baby names. Chile, New Zealand, Denmark, Portugal, Germany, France, and Iceland are examples. In 2009, the judge José Ángel Aquino from the Dominican Republic submitted without success a resolution to ban names that were "derogatory, extravagant or vulgar such as those used to refer to body parts, brands, commercial names, science fiction characters, offensive words, among others." With this project, the judge attempted to prohibit names like "Bobona Guerrero de los Santos, Tonton Ruiz, Adicto de los Santos, Seno Jiménez, Ernesto Che Pérez, Winston Churchill de la Cruz, John F. Kennedy Santana (and) Rambo Mota."[1]

In the January 14th, 2012 issue of The Economist an article was published on government regulations regarding baby names. This article makes reference to a survey made by the economists Roland Fryer and Steven Levitt that conclude "that nearly 30% of black girls in California in the 1990s received a first name that they share with no other baby born in the state in the same year". In my opinion, something similar could be happening in Puerto Rico.

I haven't found any formal study of this practice on the Island, but there are some comments in the media about it. Press articles have state some of the difficulties created by "inventing" a name:

   1. You cannot distinguish if it is a boy or a girl name.

   2. The child will have difficulties learning how to write his/her name.

   3. Bullying.

   4. Official document mistakes that could lead to denying the validation of a document or extra charges to correct them.

But none of these arguments are good enough to stop the creativity of the *Boricuas*. In my opinion, it is totally valid that the parents have a desire to have a unique and special name for their child. At the end of the day, the kid will have both their genes and it is so fascinating that the name is a reflection of that.

---

[1] Source: **Proyecto prohibe nombres raros.** From Wapa.tv on April 21, 2009.
http://www.wapa.tv/noticias/especiales/proyecto_prohibe_nombres_raros_20090421175540.html

What makes a name unique?

For this book I have identified the following methods of arriving at a baby's name:

1. Two or more names combined. (Example: Ana + Natalia = Anatalia, Jared + Diana = Jariana, Karla + Lissette = Karlaissette)

2. Alternate ways to write a common name. (Example: Jessika for Jessica, Karmen for Carmen, Alanys for Alanis)

3. A totally new creation. (Example: Keidaliz, Zoidariam)

4. Names that were made popular because of the media exposure. (Example: Tanairí, Shakira, Yandel)

5. Names used by past generations, but that are not popular anymore. (Example: Ruperta, Petronila)

6. Borrow the name from a well known word, perhaps without even realizing it. Within this book you will find names from a brand of chocolate, a State in the United States, an African city, a brand of body cream, a famous Muppet, a car model and a country.

Names of Saints

This practice of young parents creating names is the main content of this book, but there are also non-common names in adults. Why? In past generations, the selection of a baby's name was often decided according to the Saint of the Day. This was a tradition in Catholic countries. Catholics follow the Liturgical Calendar that gives the dates when a Saint is honored. Since there are approximately 10,000 saints or candidates awaiting sainthood, there is more than one option for every day of the year. For example, if I were born 70 years ago –in the times of my grandparents or great grandparents- in Puerto Rico, my name could have been be Godeleva, Julita, Leopolda or Ursa. But don't worry, if your baby is born on July 30th and you want to follow this Catholic tradition there are other options such as Josefina or María. Now-a-days this tradition is no longer practiced in Puerto Rico.

Celebrity Names or Mistakes

Besides using current names to create new ones, Puerto Ricans use celebrity names, just as happens in other countries. For instance, the name of the reggaeton singer Yandel from the musical group Wisin & Yandel entered the Social Security most common names list in 2003 just when his career started taking off. In that year 49 boys were registered with his name and continuous growth every subsequent year through 2006 when it peaked at 96 boys registered. After that, the amount of boys named Yandel has been lowering, but is still on the list of the most popular with 45 boys registered in 2010. We don't know why his fellow partner Wisin didn't achieve the same because his name is not even mentioned on the lists. This example is very funny for me because Yandel is just an artistic name.

There are also uncommon names created by accident and the best story that illustrates this is my sister Analiza. Yes, she is the only person I know that has a name that is a verb (translation: Analize). My parents' idea was to name her Ana Lisa, but the person in the Demographic Registrar's office wrote her name incorrectly.

Even though there is this trend of creating new names, the "traditional" names are still more popular. For example, according to information of the Social Security Administration –that reports separate name statistic for Puerto Rico- during the last 12 years the Number One name for a boy is Luis. For girls, the favorite is Alondra that is always in the Top 5 every year.

We hope this compilation stimulates and sparks the creativity of you as new parents to find the ideal name for your baby. We don't pretend to study the origin and meaning of each name in this book. *Baby Names from Puerto Rico* celebrates the uniqueness of each person by providing ideas to name others. Enjoy this ever-so-important step in your baby's life!

Diana

BABY NAMES FOR GIRLS

A

Abdielys
Abeida
Abellemarie
Abiliz
Abinely
Abinery
Abisay
Abynalie
Adabel
Adagilsa
Adair
Adalgisa
Adali
Adalis
Adalisse
Adaliz
Adalyz
Adamila

Adamin
Adanys
Adarelys
Adarminda
Adarys
Adavel
Adbely
Addis
Adeivettlissa
Adelinzy
Adeliris
Adelis
Adelma
Adelmarie
Adelyn
Ademaris
Ademir
Adenit
Adializ
Adianez

Adianisse
Adianiz
Adiary
Adieren
Adilén
Adimarie
Adinorath
Adleen
Adlene
Adlín
Adnerys
Adolfina
Adria
Adrialy
Adriannette
Adriel
Adrienne
Adyanette
Aeleen
Aelin

Agapita	Alanys	Allymaris
Agar	Albalisis	Allysha
Agmarie	Alberticia	Almarie
Agracelia	Alda	Alodia
Agracelis	Aldiana	Aloidy
Agripina	Aleidys	Alrys
Aidaline	Aleisha	Altemira
Aidalis	Aleishka	Alvilda
Aidalisse	Aleja	Aly
Aidelisa	Alejandrina	Alynell
Aideliz	Alejita	Alys
Aidelmy	Alexa	Alyssa
Aidil	Alexi	Alyxa
Aidimarie	Alexlyane	Alyzoet
Aidiness	Aleyda	Amahira
Aidza	Aleysha	Amairy
Ailed	Aliangie	Amalie
Ailenid	Alianys	Amalyn
Ailiana	Alichia	Amantina
Ailyn	Aliesha	Amarelis
Airaliz	Alimaris	Amareliz
Aireene	Alimarys	Amarelys
Airín	Aliris	Amberleigh
Aisha	Alishber	Ambrosía
Aitza	Alissa	Amedaris
Aixa	Alizaida	Amerilys
Aizleen	Alizay	Amestry
Aiztinel	Alizbeth	Amina
Alannah	Alleen	Amirelis

Amneris
Anaceli
Anacelis
Anadith
Anaeli
Anai
Anaid
Anaida
Anaika
Anaili
Anairahe
Anaiska
Analix
Analiz
Analiza
Analy
Analyis
Anastacha
Anatalia
Anatolia
Anayancy
Anayda
Anayma
Anayris
Anca
Andrealiz
Andreily
Andri
Aneida

Anel
Anelisa
Anellys
Aneris
Aneshka
Angee
Angelee
Angelik
Angelique
Angelitza
Angelivette
Angeliz
Angely
Angelys
Angenida
Angiliz
Angivette
Ania
Aniceta
Anid
Anitah
Anitza
Anixa
Anjuliette
Anmar
Annelisse
Anneris
Annexaida
Annick

Annielith
Annjoslys
Annyoly
Antolina
Antuanette
Anyelys
Anyrsa
Apolonia
Aracelia
Aradys
Araminta
Aramita
Aranyelis
Arbilia
Arcelia
Arcilia
Ardyce
Areidy
Aremelis
Areyssa
Argynis
Ariadna
Ariagna
Arialy
Ariam
Ariana
Ariannis
Arianys
Ariaska

Aribel
Aricelis
Arisleida
Arisleyda
Aritssa
Ariyaid
Arlin
Arlynee
Armenia
Arsenia
Artdalis
Arwen
Arwinda
Ary
Aryamid
Arylis
Asenet
Ashanti
Ashely
Ashlean
Ashlie
Ashly
Ashlye
Ashnick
Asley
Aslin
Aslyn
Aspacia
Athziry

Atilana
Atneida
Audalina
Audeliz
Audelizbeth
Audrette
Audrey
Aurea Betty
Aurelie
Aurelis
Aurilda
Auronelis
Aury
Avis
Awanda
Axa
Axciades
Axely
Axenette
Ayeisha
Ayholany
Aylliana
Aysha
Ayvialis
Azalia
Azarel
Azaria
Azsa
Aztrid

Azziza

B

Babelyn
Basilia
Basilides
Basilisa
Basthy
Baudilia
Bebalis
Beira
Beisaliz
Belangie
Belanna
Beledis
Beleniris
Belerma
Belisa
Belitza
Beliza
Belkis
Belky
Belybeth
Benalis
Benjalyn
Berenice
Berlitz

Bermaly
Bernardita
Bernice
Berniss
Bernnysse
Bersy
Bertty
Bess
Bessie
Bessy
Bethania
Bethmarie
Bethsaida
Bethzaily
Bethzaley
Betsayra
Betzaida
Betzalie
Betzamabeth
Betzangely
Betzi
Betzmarie
Betzy
Betzzabeth
Bevelyn
Bexaida
Bexanda
Beyra
Bezaida

Bezlyn
Bisset
Bitia
Blasina
Bonifacia
Branda
Braulia
Brendalee
Brendali
Brendalis
Brendaliz
Brendaly
Brendalys
Brendy
Brendymar
Breseline
Brialis
Briana
Briceyra
Bridgiana
Brildalis
Brinesca
Brisdelin
Briseida
Brisneydi
Britzeida
Brizaida
Brumali
Buenaventura

C

Cadeniris
Calisha
Calixta
Candy
Cannie
Cantalicia
Caonina
Carail
Cared
Carelis
Carelys
Carenly
Carian
Carianna
Caribelle
Carilia
Carilyn
Carimarie
Carin
Carinel
Carismely
Carissa
Carleris
Carlina
Carlysmary
Carmen
Carol

Carrie
Cartalicia
Carybelle
Caryl
Carymar
Casilda
Casimira
Castora
Castula
Cateline
Cathia
Catiela
Catili
Caxandra
Cayita
Ceferina
Celady
Celedonia
Celenia
Celenita
Celeny
Celesmarie
Celiadenisse
Celibette
Celidez
Celinda
Celis
Celisse
Cesiah

Cesiannette
Cesil
Chailyn
Chaira
Chakira
Chamir
Chanelli
Chaniedid
Chantee
Chanty
Charelly
Charetsee
Charibel
Charilaisa
Charilin
Charilys
Charin
Charis
Charitín
Charito
Charitza
Charleen
Charlene
Charlensie
Charlyn
Charmaine
Charolyn
Chary
Charymar

Charys
Chasity
Chayra
Cheila
Chely
Chemillie
Chenia
Cheresada
Cherith
Cherlie
Cherlyn
Cheryliz
Cheska
Chevita
Chianese
Chiara
Chiedza
Chrirty
Chrisangelly
Chrisdaliz
Chrismarie
Cilia
Ciliamar
Cindia
Cindymar
Cinthya
Ciomara
Circe
Cire

Civette
Claraitza
Claridia
Clarisell
Clarivel
Clarivette
Clary
Clarymarie
Claudina
Claudy
Cleidy
Cleofe
Cleofina
Clisanta
Clotilde
Conchita
Conda
Confesora
Conorada
Conrada
Coral
Coralia
Coralisse
Corín
Corintia
Corliss
Cornelia
Coronada
Cory

Crecencia
Cresce
Crescencia
Crisalida
Criseida
Crismarli
Crismely
Crissandra
Cristobalina
Cristydian
Cruzaira
Cylinda
Cyndia

D

Dabatha
Dachira
Dacmaris
Dagmari
Dagmarie
Dagmaris
Dagmary
Dahiana
Daiam
Daiana
Daibelis
Daileen

Daily
Dailyn
Daina
Daines
Dairla
Dairyn
Daisi
Daisinette
Daisyre
Daisyrey
Daknes
Dalba
Dalianies
Dalibeth
Dalieli
Dalila
Dalinet
Daliris
Dalis
Dalissa
Dalitza
Daliza
Dalmarie
Dalmariel
Dalmemar
Dalysomayra
Dalytza
Damalis
Damalit

Damari	Danila	Dashia
Damarie	Danilly	Dashira
Damarilys	Danisha	Daslin
Damaristua	Danisher	Dasmin
Damarith	Danitzia	Datchira
Damary	Daniza	Daumarie
Damarys	Dannette	Dauneris
Damasa	Danniebelle	Daveiry
Damayra	Dannise	Dayalí
Damiana	Danyz	Dayana
Damilsa	Daphne	Dayane
Damily	Daphnee	Dayaneries
Damir	Darelis	Dayaneris
Damira	Dariancy	Dayanna
Damirelys	Dariangie	Daybelis
Danaliz	Darianis	Dayl
Daneida	Darielys	Daylin
Daneira	Darilyn	Dayline
Danelis	Darinette	Dayna
Danelly	Darisabel	Daynie
Danelys	Darisbel	Daysi
Daneris	Daritza	Dazlyn
Danese	Darla	Debrah
Daneska	Darleen	Debyan
Danessa	Darling	Dedzaida
Danet	Dary	Deelores
Danette	Daryana	Deida
Dania	Darys	Deidre
Danielys	Dasha	Deilly

Delaila
Delgadina
Delianamar
Deliann
Delinette
Delis
Delish
Delith
Delka
Delly
Delma
Delorean
Delsy
Delta
Delthy
Delyssa
Demetria
Dendadiarena
Denese
Denia
Denice
Denise
Denisha
Denisia
Denisse
Denitza
Denizaira
Dennise
Dennisse

Denys
Derisel
Derly
Deserie
Desidere
Desiret
Desmarie
Dessire
Destiny
Desyrel
Deurcisia
Deximary
Dayanara
Deyanara
Deyanira
Deymis
Deyshka
Dhaime
Dhalma
Dharna
Diadeliz
Diahne
Dialis
Dialma
Diamaris
Diamarys
Diamis
Dianalexia
Dianeliz

Dianellie
Dianeska
Dianette
Dianilda
Dianisa
Dianishia
Dianivette
Dianneris
Diannie
Dianoly
Diara
Didmarie
Diega
Dilania
Dilcia
Dileana
Dilenia
Dilfia
Dilian
Dilma
Dilubina
Dima
Dimara
Dimari
Dimarie
Dimaris
Dimary
Dimarys
Dimas

Dimayra
Dinaris
Dindiana
Dinnellia
Diodaris
Diodexis
Diógenes
Diolide
Diolinet
Diomara
Diomaris
Diomarys
Diomedes
Dionicia
Dionisia
Dionneelly
Dioris
Dipsa
Disnarda
Dolymar
Domitila
Donelly
Donivel
Donny
Doraliz
Dorany
Dorayma
Dorca
Dorcas

Dorcy
Dori
Dorián
Doriana
Doriann
Dorianne
Doricel
Doriliz
Dorimar
Dorinly
Doris
Doritza
Dorka
Dorkaida
Dorline
Drisbely
Dsharonli
Dubilina
Duliana
Dycmarie
Dyddian
Dyhalma
Dylmaries
Dymarie
Dymaris
Dyraida

E

Earleen
Ebineli
Edelmira
Ederly
Edermira
Edibeth
Ediburga
Edicenia
Edilberta
Edilburga
Edivette
Edliannie
Edma
Edmarie
Edmary
Edmee
Edmilly
Ednaseth
Eduarda
Eduvige
Eduviges
Eduvigis
Eduvijes
Efigenia
Efni
Egda
Egelia

Eida	Eliannette	Elizmaried
Eidimar	Eliany	Ellery
Einar	Elianys	Ellis
Einybel	Eliasendra	Elmarys
Eira	Elidia	Elmis
Eiramyle	Elienid	Eloida
Eislee	Elienis	Eloina
Eítza	Eliet	Eloísa
Eladia	Elijinet	Eloyda
Elamar	Elilia	Elpidia
Elbina	Elimar	Elsiedelia
Elcira	Elimarie	Elsy
Elda	Elines	Elva
Eledigia	Elinette	Elvia
Eledys	Elis	Ely
Eleida	Elisandra	Elydia
Eleines	Elisaura	Elymarie
Eleneida	Elisina	Elynnette
Eleniel	Elisita	Elyris
Elenn	Elisivette	Elyse
Eleny	Elismarie	Elyvette
Elercia	Elissoned	Emelee
Elgui	Eliz	Emeleen
Eliadiz	Elizabele	Emelia
Eliana	Elizabet	Emelin
Elianette	Elizabethe	Emelina
Elianis	Elizaida	Emelinda
Eliann	Elized	Emeline
Elianne	Elizet	Emely

Emelyn
Emeri
Emerida
Emeris
Emérita
Emilen
Emilette
Emilie
Emilse
Emiluz
Emilys
Emimar
Emine
Emmarie
Emmarien
Emmy
Emmyliss
Emsey
Emy
Emycel
Enadilis
Enaida
Endy
Enegza
Eneris
Engracia
Enherlinda
Enidsa
Eniks

Enis
Eniser
Enith
Enitt
Enriquelina
Enriqueta
Envelisse
Épica
Epifania
Epimenia
Eraida
Ercilia
Erenia
Éricka
Eridania
Erimir
Erleen
Erlinda
Ermelinda
Erminelly
Ernestina
Erohilda
Eroida
Ervin
Escolástica
Eselyn
Esined
Esmailyn
Esperancita

Estebania
Estefani
Estefany
Estelle
Estevania
Esthephany
Estrervina
Etanisla
Etienne
Etniz
Eudosia
Eufemia
Euladis
Eulalia
Eulogia
Eusebia
Eusobia
Eustacia
Eustaquia
Eutemia
Evalisha
Evaliz
Evanesse
Evangelina
Evangeline
Evangelista
Evangelita
Evangelly
Evangels

Evangely
Evarista
Evelia
Evelidys
Evelis
Evelissa
Evelisse
Evelitza
Eveliz
Everedith
Evergista
Everlidis
Everlidys
Evet
Evette
Evies
Evineliss
Evonny
Evysh
Exmirna
Exsuanette
Eylanne
Eymard
Eyris
Ezequiela

F

Falinda
Fancy
Fanny
Fara
Farha
Fátima
Fausta
Faustina
Faviola
Felicia
Felícita
Felipa
Felmari
Ferey
Fermina
Fideily
Fidencia
Filomena
Filomera
Fily
Fior
Fiordaliza
Fiorela
Flavia
Flerida
Florange
Florangelis

Florarminda
Flordeliz
Florentina
Florimar
Florita
Fortuna
Franceline
Francesca
Franchaska
Francheliz
Franchellie
Franchesca
Francheska
Franchezca
Franci
Francia
Francibeth
Francine
Francisca
Francisgina
Francoise
Francys
Franlisse
Franshelis
Fransheslie
Fransualis
Fredeswinda
Frenchy
Freyda

G

Gabrieliz
Gadelyn
Gala
Gamary
Gaudy
Geesel
Geisa
Geisha
Geiza
Gelanie Anid
Gelin
Gelinette
Gelliann
Gelsy
Gelymar
Genevieve
Genoveva
Genovie
Gentzabel
Georgeana
Georgina
Georyanna
Geovanna
Geralda
Geraldita

Geranid
Gerarda
Gerardina
Gerenalda
Gerlyn
Germana
Germarie
Germaris
Germiene
Germyn
Gernabelle
Geronima
Gerryan
Gertrudis
Gesilenia
Getza
Gezette Marie
Gheidys
Ghia
Giancara
Gianka
Gianna
Giannina
Gileska
Gillesy
Gilmarie
Gilvelisse
Gina
Gineris

Ginessa
Ginette
Gineyra
Ginnette
Ginny
Giohannie
Giomarie
Giomary
Gionira
Giorelix
Giosanny
Gira
Gisel
Gisellemarie
Giselly
Giselys
Gissely
Gisselys
Gisuel
Gitza
Gizelle
Gizet
Gladines
Gladixsa
Gladyann
Gladynel
Gladynelle
Glaishma
Glamarys

Glanidsa
Glaricelis
Glaris
Glarysel
Gledia
Glendali
Glendalis
Glendaliz
Glendaly
Glendalys
Glendy
Glenlybeth
Glenn Marie
Glenny
Gleny Yesen
Glenyamiles
Glewyndaliz
Glicelle
Glised
Glizette
Gloreinne
Gloriamary
Glorian
Glorianette
Gloriannie
Gloribee
Gloribel
Gloribeth
Glorie

Glorieliz
Glorietty
Gloriluz
Glorilyn
Glorimely
Glorina
Glorinette
Glorisel
Gloriselle
Gloritza
Glorivee
Glorivel
Glorivelisse
Glorivette
Glorivianne
Gloromilda
Glorrianne
Gloryangeli
Gloryann
Glorybel
Glorybell
Glorylee
Glorymar
Glorymir
Glorynes
Glorysmali
Gloryved
Gloryvee
Gloryvette

Gonzala
Govinda
Gracesha
Gracezabeth
Graciaodette
Gracielina
Gracielli
Gracielly
Graciliana
Gramelia
Grecia
Gregoria
Greicy
Gresylene
Gretchene
Gretcher
Gretmarie
Gretshen
Gretza
Gretzel
Gretzie Jan
Greycha Marie
Greysha
Greyssa
Gricel
Gricelia
Gricelis
Gricelle
Grimaldi

Grimarys
Grisdeliz
Grisel
Griser
Grisheyla
Grismarie
Grisolette
Grizaida
Grizert
Grizette
Grysseyliz
Gudelia
Gueisha
Guelmarie
Guelymar
Guimary
Gumercinda
Gumersinda
Gurian Marie
Gwendely Dazlyn
Gwendolyn
Gydashky
Gymari
Gynna
Gysela

H

Haddel

Haddy
Haidee
Haidy
Haizel
Halima
Harhisha
Haydie
Haymet
Headdie
Hebe
Hecdalis
Hecdys Joan
Heciris
Hecmarelis
Hecmarie
Hecmary
Hectlys
Heida
Heiddy
Heidie
Heidy
Heileen
Heily
Heilyn
Heisa
Heisha Marie
Helga
Helia
Hellitz

Helvetia
Herdil
Herica
Herma
Hermarie
Hermenegilda
Hermogene
Hermógenes
Hermy Idalia
Herodis
Heroilda
Heyda
Heydalexa
Heysel
Heysha
Higinia
Hilcias
Hildamaris
Hildelisa
Hilsa
Hilvia
Himilce
Hipólita
Hiraida
Hiramilis
Hiriana
Honoria
Horialis

I

Ibelimary
Iberelis
Ibeth
Ibis
Ida
Idabell
Idali
Idalia
Idalice
Idalie
Idalina
Idalis
Idalise
Idalissa
Idalisse
Idaliz
Idaliza
Idalme
Idalmis
Idalmy
Idalys
Idamar
Idamaris
Idangelic
Idangely
Idanis
Idaris Enid

Idary
Idasel
Idelisa
Idelisse
Ideliz
Ideliza
Idesse
Idette Yarixa
Idis
Idith
Idolina
Idualys
Igmarie
Ignarda
Ignasia
Igris
Igsi
Ilca
Ildna
Ileaneth
Ileanett
Ileanexi
Ileanexis
Ileangelis
Ileis
Ilene
Ilia Nitsa
Iliam
Ilianette

Ilka
Illelipsy
Illian
Illiane
Ilsia
Iluminada
Ilvya
Imalay
Imeida
Imerda
Imirllari
Ina
Ineabell
Ineabelle
Inelis
Inelisse
Inginia
Iniabel
Iniabelle
Init
Inmarie
Inocencia
Iolda
Iomarys
Irache
Iraima
Iralys
Iramia
Irany

Ircha
Ireliz
Irelys
Irenda
Irens
Iriacnet
Irian
Iriany
Iricel
Irisbel
Irisbell
Iriselis
Irish Betzy
Irisjan
Irmalis
Irmarie
Irmarilis
Irmaris
Irvia Idalie
Irvian
Isadayri
Isaeileen
Isaleanet
Isamar
Isamarie
Isamary
Isare
Isbeel
Isel

Isela
Isell
Isern
Ishataimmy
Ishell
Isila
Isis
Isisnachelly
Ismaiet
Ismari
Ismarie
Ismary
Istia
Itsamar
Itza
Itzahyana
Itzaira
Itzamar
Itzary
Ivana
Ivanelysse
Ivania
Ivanid
Ivannette
Ivanska
Ivelis
Ivelises
Ivelissa
Ivelisse

Iveliza
Ivelys
Ivessika
Ivia
Ivismarie
Ivonnette
Ixa
Ixaivia
Ixchel
Ixeanely
Ixia
Izaidy Beth
Izeris
Izomalee

J

Jaced
Jacelyn
Jacinta
Jackelin
Jackeline
Jackelyne
Jackiline
Jackleen
Jackmary
Jackseline
Jaclyn

Jaclyn Gisuel
Jadeline
Jadira
Jaedy
Jael
Jaeleen
Jaelynn
Jaemilyn
Jahaira
Jahgen
Jahomy
Jaileen
Jailene
Jailine
Jailyn
Jailynne
Jaimarie
Jaimie
Jainiés
Jaítza
Jaizel
Jalexandra
Jalimar
Jamaris
Jamarys
Jameris
Jamesie
Jamie
Jamilette

Jammilah
Jammile
Jan
Jancie
Jancy
Janedith
Janeisy
Janeixa
Janelee
Janelise
Janeliz
Janelle
Janelly
Janellys
Janelys
Janeniris
Janeri
Janeris
Janerys
Jani
Jania
Janibiz
Janice Japhire
Janiece
Janiellys
Janielys
Janilette
Janina
Janine

Janira
Janiraliz
Janitza
Janitzy
Janmarily
Janna Milena
Jannely
Jannilly
Jansenny
Janyll
Janzmari
Japhire
Jaranaiza
Jarelis
Jarelisse
Jaribet
Jarielys
Jariette
Jaritza
Jarivette
Jarlin
Jarlyn
Jasais
Jashai Annette
Jashira
Jashira Marie
Jasmelly
Jasminda
Jasmira

Jaychaliz	Jeilymar	Jennifer Lynn
Jayleen	Jeilyn	Nasira
Jaylene	Jeimily	Jennifred
Jaylin	Jeimimar	Jennis
Jaylinette	Jeini	Jennisbeth
Jaymarie	Jeisa	Jennise
Jaymie	Jeissa	Jennylee
Jaysa	Jekamil	Jennylin
Jazmira	Jelice	Jennyliz
Jeami	Jelis	Jennyloo
Jeanelie	Jelisa	Jenyeira
Jeanelly	Jelissa	Jericka
Jeaneska	Jelitsa	Jeritza
Jeanetsie	Jelitza	Jeroline
Jeanette	Jellixza	Jerónima
Jeanie	Jem	Jesaira
Jeanmarie	Jenauny	Jesamary
Jeanna	Jenerssi	Jeselyn
Jeanne Ivette	Jeniann	Jesena
Jeannelis	Jenie	Jesika
Jeannette	Jeniliz	Jesimar
Jeannyra	Jenille	Jesinette
Jeara	Jenillee	Jesinia
Jeassy	Jenimar	Jesivette
Jedith	Jenipher	Jeslie
Jeenher	Jenissa	Jesly
Jeika	Jenitza	Jesmarie
Jeileen	Jennette	Jesmary
Jeillyn	Jennie	Jesselle

Jessena	Jinitza	Jocelyn
Jessica Zadiel	Jinneiry	Jocelyne
Jessika	Jinny	Jochebed
Jessline	Jipsy Marie	Joelia
Jessmarie	Jiselle	Joelian
Jesusa	Jiselly	Joelly
Jesussa	Jissela	Joely
Jethzabelle	Jisselle	Joemily
Jetsenia	Jisselys	Joen
Jetsybell	Jissette	Joeny Marie
Jetzabel	Joaly	Joesmari
Jexenia	Joam	Jogalys
Jeylene	Joamilette	Johalicen
Jeyliz	Joan	Johalys
Jeyra	Joana	Johanis
Jeysa	Joanette	Johanit
Jeysha	Joanly	Johannah
Jezabel	Joanmarie	Johannie
Jhaitza	Joann	Johannis
Jhancy	Joanna	Johanny Marie
Jhanis	Joanne	Johany
Jhanitza	Joannette	Johanys
Jickys	Joannie	Johayra
Jienny	Joannne	Joheinys
Jillia	Joanny	Johenid
Jimmelizabeth	Joanska	Joivelisse
Jinan	Joany	Jolene
Jinet	Joaquina	Jolymar
Jinette	Joarelia	Jomaira

Jomally

Jomara

Jomarie

Jomary

Jomarys

Jomayra

Jondaly

Jonely

Jorannie

Jorgila

Jorisabel

Jormarie

Josaira

Josaranie

Josefa

Josey Mirelys

Jossie

Jossimarye

Jossmarie

Jossy

Josynel

Joura

Jovalise

Jovana

Jovanka

Jovanna

Jovanny

Jovina

Jovita

Joyce Marie

Joyceneidy

Joyse

Juary

Jubilmar

Judcel

Judis

Judit

Judithssan

Judymar

Juliany

Julianys

Julibeth

Julicell

Juliesa

Juliette

Julievette

Julimar

Julinés

Julissa

Julisvette

Julitza

Julivette

Julyssa

Junaira

Junian

Junitza

Jurizan

Jusmary

Justacia

Juvetzy

K

Kacie Cherlyn

Kaholy

Kailine

Kairiana

Kaishla

Kaislah

Kaitlyn

Kaleishmi

Kamalieh

Kamid

Kamil

Kamilah

Kammy

Kamy

Kaoru

Kareena

Kareliz

Karellys

Karelyn

Karelys

Karem

Karemly

Karenin

Karenina Natalia
Karenly
Karent
Kariana
Karianise
Kariann
Karidad
Karidgie
Karielly
Karielys
Karilyn
Karima
Karime
Karin
Kariowaxa
Karishna Nicole
Karislin
Karitza
Karla
Karlaissette
Karlaliz
Karleen
Karlenie
Karma
Karmarie
Karmen
Karmy
Karol
Kary

Karylin
Katany
Katheryn
Kathia Yaris
Kathie
Kathiria
Kathirya
Kathryn
Kathya
Kathyenid
Kathyria
Kathyska
Katia
Katia Marie
Katia Yari
Katia Yaris
Katia Yary
Katiana
Katianette
Katilia Marie
Katina
Katiria
Katsi
Katyriam
Kaura
Kayla
Kaylaliz
Kaysa
Kaysie

Keanny
Keidaliz
Keidy
Keila
Keilee
Keilie
Keilyn
Keimalys
Keira
Keirisis
Keisa
Keisha
Keishla
Keishla Dessire
Keishmary
Keishmer
Keisla
Keisy
Keisy Denisse
Keixha
Keiza
Kelitza
Kelly Janellys
Kellymel
Kelmy
Kendra
Kenelma
Kenia
Kenia Lee

Kenira	Khitsy	Kisha
Kenthya	Khyrsis	Kisha Amneris
Kenuelys	Khyrsys	Kisha Zoe
Keren	Kiara Lee	Kissairis
Kesha	Kiara Lis	Kithiasoet
Keshia	Kiara Marie	Kizai
Kesly	Kiaralis	Klaribell
Kessiria	Kiaraliz	Klariss
Ketsia	Kiarely	Koral
Ketsy	Kichayra Lee	Koralys
Ketty	Kienny	Krimhilda
Keycha	Kildean	Krisbel
Keyla	Kilsey	Krismar
Keyla Liz	Kimberlie	Krismerry
Keylee	Kimberline	Kristaly
Keylene	Kimberlys	Kristhia
Keylisa	Kimeris	Kristia
Keymarie	Kimet	Kristina
Keyna	Kimitzia	Kristtia
Keyra	Kiomara	Kritzeli
Keysha	Kiomarie	Krizcia
Keysha Yesenia	Kiomarilyn	Krizia
Keyshla	Kiomary	Krysmari
Keyshla Katiria	Kiomery	Krystal Lynn
Keyshla Zoe	Kiria	Krystel
Keyshly	Kiriath	Krystle
Keysla	Kirsi	Kryzia
Kharem	Kirstielynn	Kylean
Khenia	Kirsy	Kymberlin

Kyriat Charis

L

Lacila
Lackechia
Lady
Lahis
Lained
Lalishka
Lalybeth
Lamacristina
Lamaris
Lanny
Lary Enid
Latisha
Laudelina
Lauratell
Laureanne
Laurelys
Lavignia
Lavinia
Layda
Lazara
Lazarett
Leadys Nelia
Leanette
Leanora

Lebiram
Leda
Ledys
Leemagdali
Leexandra
Leeziy
Leginska Yahymara
Legna
Leichlany
Leichlim
Leidy
Leilani
Leilanis
Leilany
Leimar
Leira
Leisally
Leixa
Lenaly
Lenibeth
Lenna Sogeily
Lennis
Lenny Esther
Lenys Mireya
Leocadia
Leomaris
Leonarda
Leoncia
Leonides

Leorgia
Lercy
Lerma
Lerys
Lesbia
Lesby Winda
Leshliane
Leslian
Lesliebel
Lessuan
Lesvia
Letty
Letty Joan
Leyda Rosana
Leyka Yenetza
Leyniska
Leynna
Leyra
Leyshla
Liadys
Liamys
Liana
Lianabel
Lianely
Lianett
Lianette
Lianette Iliam
Lianibeth
Liannelys

Liany
Liboria
Librada
Liceliz
Licelott
Licet
Licialy
Licy
Lidelisse
Lidelys
Lidianne
Lidice
Lidied
Lidiette
Lidrada
Lidubina
Liduvina
Lidy
Liesel
Liestchen
Liety
Ligia
Ligny
Ligsia
Lilin
Lilmarie
Lilybeth
Limar
Lindemar

Lineethe
Linel
Lingerie
Linneidy
Linnete
Linnette
Lirca
Lirimar
Lisaira
Lisanaeli
Lisandy
Lisangela
Lisaura
Lisbelle
Lisela
Lisell
Liset
Lisnel
Lissuannette
Litshaivette
Litzaida
Litzi
Livette
Lixalis
Lixlia
Liz Yinellys
Lizaida
Lizalee
Lizanne

Lizaries
Lizayra
Lizbel Cristina
Lizbenette
Lizceidy
Lizdalia
Lizdeika
Lizdianel
Lizeida
Lizelyn
Lizmaira
Lizmeliz
Liznei
Liznel
Liznelly
Liznelt
Llarilys
Llomar
Llovianska
Loaiza
Loanda
Loira
Loiz
Lolibeth
Longina
Longira
Loraima
Lorelei
Lorell

Loren
Lorenza
Loriam
Loriann
Lorimar
Lorka
Lormariel
Lornyvette
Lorraine
Loruhama
Louana
Lourdeliz
Lourrienn Gisel
Loyma
Lubelmarri
Lucelenia
Lucelian
Lucette
Lucina
Lucinda
Lucinette
Lucydalies
Ludivina
Ludovina
Ludwina
Luisel
Luisette
Lulda
Lumari

Lumaris
Lumary
Lurmar
Lusandy
Lusely
Luvana
Luz Adelma
Luz Celenia
Luzbel
Luzbeth
Luzeika
Luzeni
Luznatalee
Luzuannette
Lyanis Marie
Lychmarie
Lydia Eulalia
Lydianet
Lydibelle
Lydiet
Lydimarie
Lydinés
Lymari
Lymarie
Lymaris
Lymary
Lymarys
Lynda
Lynelis

Lynissa
Lynnes
Lynoshka
Lysandra
Lysbeth
Lyset
Lyska
Lysmarie
Lysmaris
Lysset
Lyssette
Lyssie
Lysvette
Lyther
Lyumma
Lyzandra
Lyzvette

M

Mabed
Mabel Aimeé
Madalis
Madeli
Madeling
Madelyne
Madian
Madilin

Mady	Malta	Margy
Maeline	Maradalis	Mari Teody
Magali	Maralice	María Ercilia
Magalis	Maralis	María Idali
Magaly	Maraliz	María Jovina
Magalys	Marangeli	María Nelsida
Magdalis	Marangelie	María Otilia
Magdaly	Marangelly	María Virgen
Magdaris	Marangely	Mariabel
Magdelis	Maranyelis	Mariadelys
Magdilis	Marari	Mariam Joely
Mahali	Marcelly	Mariame
Mahalia	Marciana	Mariamjuly
Mahaly	Marcola	Mariamlly
Mahelet	Marcolina	Marianellis
Maibelis	Marcybeth	Marianett
Maibeliz	Mared	Mariangelí
Maida	Mareisa	Mariangelie
Maidaly	Mareli	Mariangelis
Mailene	Marelis	Mariangely
Mairilys	Marella	Mariangelys
Mairim	Marelyn	Marianyelin
Mairym	Marena	Marianyili
Malenie	Margalyz	Maricelli
Maleny	Margety	Marichelle
Maletsis	Marggie	Maricsa
Malini	Margi	Maridelis
Malixza	Margielette	Marie Zulma
Mallory	Margorie	Marielix

Marieliz	Marlene	Megdalea
Mariellys	Marlín	Meileen
Marielmi	Marline	Meiling
Mariely	Marlis	Meiryn
Marielys	Marlyn	Meisy
Mariesely	Martaivonne	Melaney
Mariher	Marva Lee	Melani
Marilaida	Mary Cheila	Melania
Marimonsi	Marybet	Melaries
Marinés	Maryland	Melba
Marinesly	Maryliam	Melbadelise
Marinly	Marylisabet	Meleiny
Marioli	Marytte	Melianyelit
Marioly	Masail	Melissa
Marirssa	Massa	Melita
Marisa	Maura	Melitza
Marisel	Mavelyn	Meliza
Mariselix	Maximina	Melmary
Mariset	Mayda	Mency
Marisoliz	Mayelin	Merab
Marissa	Mayeling	Meralys
Maritza	Mayelinne	Meralys Soleil
Marivelisse	Mayleen	Merania
Marivette	Maylix	Merari
Marixabel	Mayrobie	Merarie
Marizaida	Maysun	Merarys
Marizol	Mayza Luz	Mergies
Marjorie Crystal	Medelicia	Meriland
Marleen	Medelisia	Merlix

Merly

Mersa Ivette

Merva

Mervaliz

Meryanne

Merylane

Meryssa

Meycy

Micheila

Micheyka

Midali

Midaly

Midelis

Midia

Migda

Migdalí

Migna

Mignaliz

Mignelly

Migxenia

Milangie

Milayda

Milayka

Milbet

Milca

Milca Yisette

Milcaleny

Miledis

Miledy

Milena

Mileny

Milet

Mileydis

Mileyka

Mileyshla

Milianette

Milidan

Milisa

Militza

Milively

Milixsa

Milka

Milliane

Millianett

Millicent

Millicet

Millivette

Milmary

Milsabel

Milta

Miltalyz

Miluirys

Milvia

Milyrca

Mimagdy

Mimary

Mimiza

Mindelys

Minee

Minelis

Mineliz

Minelly

Minna

Minnette

Minoshka

Miosotis

Miraidaliz

Miralia

Mircia

Mireddys

Mireely

Mireidi

Mireidy

Mirelis

Mireliss

Mirella

Mirelsa

Mirely

Mirelys

Mireni

Miresel

Mireya

Mirheilen

Miria

Miriam Yamilka

Miriany

Mirka

Mirla
Mirnaliz
Miroslava
Mirta
Mirtelina
Mirtha
Mirtheschka
Mirtia
Mirza
Mishelle
Misleyda
Misol
Mitchelle
Mititza
Mitzi
Mivian
Mivlin
Mixia
Monín
Monsita
Morayma
Myanell
Mychally
Mydalis
Myleshka
Mylexia
Mylitza
Mylka
Mylmarie

Myosotis
Myra
Myraida
Myralis
Myreliz
Myriam
Myrian
Myrliana
Myrliza
Myrnaliz
Myrnelis
Myrta
Myrtelina
Myrzabel

N

Nachaira
Nachaliz
Nadeida
Nadhira
Nadhya
Nadine
Nadiuska
Nadja Noraly
Nadyalee
Nadyan
Naelis

Nahed
Nahiony
Nahir
Nahirlee
Nahivys
Nahomi
Nahomys
Naiara
Naihomie
Naikalee
Naila
Naila Milbet
Nailin
Nailyn
Nair
Nairobi
Nairobis
Nairy
Naishaly
Naitza
Naiza
Nakicha
Naldy
Nalfa
Nalissa
Nanali
Nanchelle
Naneshka
Nanishka

Nanysma	Nayla	Nelis
Nara	Naylis	Nelisa
Naraya	Naymarie	Nelismar
Narcisa	Nayra	Nelitza
Narda	Nayrimlee	Nellidiz
Nardaliz	Naysa	Nellied
Nardy	Naysha	Nellynet
Nasha	Naytsha	Nellys
Nashalí	Nechel Marie	Nelmary
Nashalie Michelle	Néctar	Nelmarys
Nashaly	Neditza	Nelsa
Nashely Suzette	Nedzabeli	Nelsida
Nasheyma	Nedzabellie	Nelsie
Nashira	Nefertiti	Nelsiel
Nasira	Neich	Nelsy
Natacha Nicol	Neida	Nelva
Natasha Yamile	Neilyan	Nelysha
Natividad	Neimy	Nemaris
Natya	Neimylis	Nemesis
Navila	Neisa	Nenuchka
Nayades	Neisha	Nerida
Nayadeth Roxana	Neitza	Neriluz
Naycha Liz	Neiyla	Nerinell
Nayeli	Nejla	Neritza
Nayelis	Nelany	Nermary
Nayeliz	Nelcie	Nerva
Nayely	Nelda	Nery
Nayhomi	Neldy	Nerylú
Naykin	Nelika	Neshmaida

Neslimar
Nesmarie
Netza
Netzy
Ney
Neyma
Neyra
Neysa
Neysha
Neyshma
Neyva
Neyvelisse
Nhakia
Niaris
Nibia
Nicanora
Nichbel
Nichet
Nichole
Nicholle Marie
Nicol
Nicolasa
Nieriv
Nigmary
Nihurka
Nilangely
Nilca
Nilda
Nildalis

Nildaly
Nildamari
Nildes
Nildy
Nilibeth
Nilis
Nilken
Nilliam
Nilma
Nilmarie
Nilmaris
Nilmary
Nilta
Nilvette
Nilvia
Nilza
Nimia
Nimsi
Nindileris
Nini
Niniveth
Ninoshka
Ninuschka
Niriam
Nirka
Nirma
Nirmaris
Nirose
Nishma

Nishmenth
Nismarie
Nita Iris
Nitzaida
Nitzali
Nitzaliz
Nitzia
Nitzy Susej
Niurka
Niushka
Niuska
Niva
Nivea
Nivia
Nivial
Nixa
Nixsaliz
Nizhah
Noanil
Noelany
Noelanys
Noelis
Noely
Noemaris
Noemirys
Noerca
Nohely
Nojely
Nolly

Nolyanne
Nomayra
Noraida
Noraima
Noralee
Noralis
Noralisse
Noraliz
Noraly
Norangely
Norayma
Norcary
Noreliz
Norelma
Norelys
Noribel
Norie
Norka
Normaliz
Normari
Normarie
Normaris
Normary
Normarys
Norymar
Noyolawilda
Nubia
Nurvidia
Nushka

Nuvia
Nycole
Nydiaam
Nydiana
Nydsy
Nyliram
Nyrka
Nyrsa
Nytzali
Nyvia

O

Obdulia
Obet
Odemarie
Odemaris
Odemarix
Odesta
Odilia
Odimar
Ogdina
Oheris
Olgalys
Olguimar
Olida
Olinda
Olpha

Omaira
Omairy
Omara
Omarilys
Omaris
Omaya
Onali Estelle
Onelia
Onellis
Ordonel
Oria
Orialis
Orializ
Orialy
Oriana Zohima
Oriann
Orlanda
Orlnim
Orosia
Orpha
Orquídea
Osilys
Otilia

P

Palvina
Pansy

Pascuala
Patsy
Patty
Paulette
Pebbles
Percida
Perfecta
Persia
Persida
Petra
Petrona
Petronila
Phaedra
Pierina
Pierrette
Porfiria
Práxedes
Primitiva
Pura
Purificación

Q

Quéndida
Quetcy
Quintina

R

Rabssarys
Rachelie
Rafmin
Rahaiza
Rahissa
Rahiza
Raisa
Raissa
Raiza
Ramelia
Ramesis
Randor
Raphet
Raquelisha
Raxelis
Rayeline
Raysa
Raysha
Rayssa
Rayza
Regalada
Reinalis
Reinaliz
Reneida
Resi
Restituta
Reymi Elizabeth

Reyneria
Rhea
Rianchell Marie
Richel
Risela
Ritangeli
Ritza
Robyannie
Rochelle
Rochelly
Roddy
Rodica
Rogelia
Roisma
Romaris
Rosael
Rosaidith
Rosaira
Rosalia
Rosalie
Rosalina
Rosalis
Rosaliz
Rosallie
Rosaly
Rosaycela
Rosayde
Rosayme
Rosemarieann

Rosemeli
Roshelly
Rosines
Rosirma
Rosiry
Rossangel
Rossed
Rossmarie
Rossymar
Rosyeimid
Rotsen
Rousaly
Rubeli
Rubencia
Ruddie
Ruddy
Rufina
Ruperta
Rutdaliz
Ruthdes

S

Saaelis
Sabeel
Saby Nelly
Sachamarie
Sachayra

Sadoyeliz
Sahily
Sahudi
Saibel
Saida
Sailin
Sailly
Saira
Sairelis
Sajire
Salvita
Salya
Samaeliz
Samaida
Samaira
Samara
Samarit
Samarivette
Samayra
Sameilia
Samirca
Samitza
Sandibel
Sandimary
Sandrali
Sandybell
Sanya
Sarahi
Saraí

Saraid
Sarangelys
Sarely
Sari
Sariany
Saribel
Saribet
Saribeth
Sarinette
Saripzia
Saritza
Sarkis
Sary
Sarybeth
Saryvette
Sasha
Sashalee
Sashly
Saturna
Saturni
Saturnina
Saudhi
Saudy
Sawally
Saya
Sayda
Saydda
Saydeth
Sayra

Sayrin
Scarlette
Scheyla
Secundina
Seferina
Selenes
Selenia
Selmarie
Selmira
Selymar
Semiramy
Senobia
Serafina
Sergida
Severa
Severeana
Shadia
Shadrim
Shaila
Shailine
Shailym
Shailyn
Shaira
Shakira
Shakyra
Shaleyka
Shalimar
Shalimst
Shalitza

Shalom
Shamary
Shamayla
Shamillette
Shandri
Shannon
Shantel
Sharely
Sharenly
Sharian
Sharifa
Sharleen
Sharlene
Sharline
Sharlyn
Sharmarie
Sharomy
Shary
Sharylan
Shauntelle
Shayna
Shayra
Sheilin
Sheily
Sheilyn
Sheilynette
Sheira
Sheiska
Shelin

Shelly
Shellymar
Shelyann
Shera Yaitza
Sherabyd
Sherell
Sheritzah
Sherlymar
Sherlyn
Sheryl
Sherys
Shevannig
Sheyla Yamina
Sheylamar
Sheylamarie
Shierly Mary
Shira
Shirally
Shirany
Shudam
Shyalala
Shynethzie
Sibia
Sigrid
Sijam
Silfida
Silka
Silka Janet
Silkia

Silmarie	Solmarie	Stephanme
Silmary	Solmary	Sthephanie
Silveria	Solmayra	Suanette
Silvestra	Solymar	Suannette
Simirna	Solymarie	Sue Haley
Sinara	Somarie	Suehati
Sindia	Sonami	Suelly
Siria	Sonibert	Suen
Siris	Sonimar	Sueseline
Sixta	Sonja	Sugeil
Soamy	Sonmarie	Sugeily
Soane	Sony	Sugein
Soangelis	Sonya	Sugey
Sobeida	Sonyvette	Suhail
Soenair	Sophia	Suhaily
Soex	Sophy	Suhalee
Sofismarie	Soralis	Suhei
Sogeily	Sorangel	Suheidy
Sojairy	Sordanela	Suheil
Soledith	Sorein	Suheilian
Soleil	Soreli	Suheily
Soleimar	Sorgalim	Suhgeil
Soleiny	Sorializ	Suineth
Solemy	Soriam	Sujei
Solibeth	Sorieliz	Sujeil
Solimar	Sorlinda	Sujeila
Solivette	Sory Ivette	Sujeilly
Solkira	Sorymar	Sujeily
Solmari	Stancy Nicole	Sujeimy

Sujeylie
Sulai
Sulaika
Sulay
Suleika
Suleil
Sulerys
Suley
Suleyka
Sulier
Sulimar
Sulinett
Sulis
Sulisaday
Suljeily
Sullay
Sullenid
Sullynett
Sulmary
Sulrey
Sureily
Surelys
Surgei
Surgey
Suria
Suriel
Surjei
Susej
Suyin

Swimary
Sybella
Sylkalianett
Sylkia
Sylmarie
Sylviamarie
Sylvianne
Syndia
Synthia

T

Tahiri
Tahis
Taimysha
Tainairy
Tainya
Tairaliz
Tairi
Taisha
Taismary
Talian
Tamahara
Tamarie
Tamesha
Tamisha
Tammy
Tanaira

Tanairí
Tanairis
Tanairiz
Tanangiela
Tanea
Tanisha Mariah
Tanya
Tanyat
Tanysha
Tarisha
Taryn
Tasha
Tashira
Taty
Tavia
Tayisha
Taymarie
Taymary
Taymi
Taysha
Teody
Terebed
Termutis
Thais
Thais Yaitza
Thaisha
Thalisha
Thamayra
Thaysha

Thirsha
Tiani
Tihanys
Tilda
Timna
Tomasa
Tomika
Tyrsha

U

Ufelina
Umberlina
Urana
Ursina
Úrsula

V

Valeriana
Valeska
Valiann
Vallerinne
Valmary
Vanexa
Vanishka
Vasthy
Vasti

Veldi
Velia
Velma
Velmaris
Velmary
Velmaryz
Venancia
Venerable
Venice
Ventura
Veralucia
Veramary
Veranis
Verenisse
Veridiana
Vernice
Vernies
Verucha
Verushka
Vethzaida
Veyda
Vianka
Vickiana
Vickiara
Victlaine
Vidalina
Vildaliz
Vilkmarie
Vilmaly

Vincky
Vinelis
Violitza
Vionette
Virgemina
Virgen Concepción
Virgen Del Milagro
Virgen Librada
Virgen Luz
Virgen María
Virgen Milagros
Virgen Rosario
Virgenmina
Virgenminia
Virna
Virtudes
Visitacion
Vitalina
Vitmarie
Vivianeth
Vivianette
Viviannette
Vynia

W

Wailí
Wailly Enith

Waldemarys
Waldetrudis
Waleska
Walexa
Walezka
Walitzia
Walkidia
Walkiria
Walory
Walquiria
Wandaline
Wandalis
Wandaliz
Wandalys
Wandeling
Wandelyne
Wayda
Wayka
Welly
Wenda
Wendalee
Wendeline
Wendeliz
Wendilee
Wendilys
Wendylis
Wesleyana
Wexly
Widalis

Widalys
Widelisse Michelle
Widnelia
Wilca
Wilda
Wildalis
Wildaliz
Wildalys
Wildelia
Wildelis
Wildelys
Wileidy
Wileyshka
Wilfidia
Wilgermina
Wilianet
Wilka
Willanys
Willeyda
Willmeliz
Wilmarie
Wilmaris
Wilmary
Wilmarys
Wilmelia
Wilmelys
Wilmery
Wilmy
Wilnelia

Wilnelly
Wilnia
Wilsabel
Wilzaida
Wina
Winda
Windy
Windyannette
Windye
Winedsy
Winelia
Winneylka
Winnie
Winsensley
Witiza
Wukiath
Wylmary
Wyneska

X

Xaimara
Xaymara
Xaymarie
Xenia
Xenia Aixa
Ximara
Xiomara
Xiomara Yadira

Xiomarie
Xiomary
Xionelys

Y

Yaceska
Yachary
Yachira
Yackeline
Yadaris
Yadelies
Yadhira
Yadibel
Yadicha Yashlyn
Yadielys Nicole
Yadimar
Yadisha
Yaditxa
Yaditza
Yadixa
Yadlin
Yaelin
Yahaira
Yahairi
Yaheiry
Yahira
Yahitza

Yahiza
Yahymara
Yaideraimi
Yaidilee
Yaidimar
Yaika Lizette
Yail
Yaileen
Yaimet
Yaira
Yairelis
Yairene
Yaisa
Yaisa Nicolle
Yaitza
Yaixa
Yaiza
Yajaira
Yajarira
Yakaira
Yakira
Yaleika
Yalessia
Yalexis Lizbeth
Yalibeth
Yalis
Yalisbeth
Yalitza
Yalreisy

Yamaira
Yamalis
Yamalyna
Yamalys
Yamara
Yamaralys
Yamarie
Yamaris
Yamary
Yamayra
Yamel
Yamelisa
Yamelyn
Yameysis
Yamila
Yamileska
Yamilet
Yamileth
Yamilett
Yamilette
Yamilie
Yamilis
Yamilka
Yamily
Yamina
Yamira
Yamirca
Yamirka
Yamirla

Yamirmarie
Yamirta
Yamitza
Yamixa
Yan
Yanaira
Yanairis
Yanara
Yancy
Yandeliz
Yanedira
Yaneida
Yanelis
Yanelly
Yaneri
Yaneris
Yanet
Yanetsy
Yanette
Yaneydi
Yani
Yanibel
Yanil
Yanila
Yanilda
Yanilee
Yanilis Limar
Yanilka
Yanilsa

Yanina
Yanina Thaís
Yaninataís
Yaniny
Yanirah
Yaniralys
Yaniris
Yaniritza
Yanis
Yanissa
Yanisse
Yanitsia
Yanitza
Yanitzia
Yannet
Yany
Yanyra
Yaqueline
Yaquira
Yara
Yarah
Yarahika
Yaralise
Yaraliz
Yaredzel
Yarelis
Yarelise
Yareliz
Yarelly

Yarellys
Yarelys
Yaremi
Yari Marie
Yarian
Yaribel
Yaribette
Yaribka
Yariel
Yarielis
Yariely
Yarietzely
Yaril
Yarilis
Yarilitza
Yarilyn
Yarilys
Yarimar
Yarimel
Yarinta
Yarira
Yaris
Yarisa
Yarisabel
Yarisbeth
Yarisel
Yarisely
Yarishna
Yarismariel

Yarisol
Yarisse
Yaritsi
Yaritza
Yarixa
Yarleen
Yarlene
Yarlin
Yarlyn
Yary
Yarynette
Yasdel
Yaseiry
Yaselie
Yaselin
Yaselis
Yashera
Yashira
Yashira Yaril
Yashline
Yashlyn
Yasilis
Yasira
Yasiris
Yaslin
Yaslyn
Yasmarieliz
Yasmil
Yasmin

Yasmira
Yasmiry
Yassiris
Yatiana
Yatsiria
Yaxsaira
Yaxyra
Yaymari
Yaysa
Yazaira
Yazdel
Yazdely
Yazeni
Yazmarie
Yazmary
Yazmillie
Yazmín
Ydarmi
Ydeen
Ydelsa
Ydzia
Yeechmarie
Yehidy
Yehimarie
Yeida
Yeidi
Yeidimar
Yeidy
Yeileen

Yeilimar
Yeiliz
Yeimari
Yeimily
Yeimy
Yeincizuhey
Yeinsemin
Yeira
Yeirah
Yeisa
Yeisabelle
Yeisicar
Yeismary
Yeismel
Yeisy
Yeitza
Yeizamar
Yelisa
Yelissa
Yelitza
Yeliza
Yelizka
Yelmaris
Yely
Yelza
Yemím
Yemzie
Yenaira
Yendry

Yenetza
Yenica
Yenifel
Yenilivette
Yenipher
Yenisca
Yenitza
Yerania
Yerardine
Yérica
Yéricka
Yérika
Yerling
Yesabelle
Yeseida
Yesen
Yeshaira
Yesibel
Yesica
Yesi
Yesika
Yeslianne
Yesmaria
Yesmarie
Yessenia
Yessica
Yessmin
Yesury
Yetzaira

Yetzenia
Yexeira
Yicella
Yilda
Yimara
Yimari
Yinellys
Yinerva
Yinet
Yinette
Yionelle
Yira
Yiralee
Yisabel
Yisel
Yiselle
Yiting
Yitzel
Yixsel
Ylen
Ylenia
Yllia
Yllian
Ylsa
Yltrebsa
Yma Angélica
Yminelis
Yoalin
Yobeida

Yodaima
Yodallys
Yodaris
Yohalyn
Yohana
Yohara
Yojeida
Yolaida
Yolane
Yolania
Yolery
Yolian
Yoliana
Yolibeth
Yolima
Yolimar
Yolimarie
Yoliner
Yoliz
Yoma
Yomaira
Yomaly
Yomara
Yomari
Yomarie
Yomaris
Yomary
Yomayra
Yonaidaliz

Yonaira
Yonaly
Yoraima
Yoriam
Yormaris
Yorvidia
Yosanie
Yoselin
Yosineydi
Yosira
Yoslin
Yosmarily
Yosmary
Youkabel
Yrrah
Yuanivel
Yuberis
Yubie
Yudelca
Yudelka
Yuleishka
Yuliana
Yuliane
Yulimar
Yulmarie
Yumaila
Yumari
Yumary
Yuriann

Yurilú
Yurineshca
Yuris
Yvelisse
Yvette
Yvonne
Yzaira
Yziz

Z

Zacha
Zachaliez
Zadiel
Zahidee
Zahily
Zahira
Zahiry
Zahrines
Zaida
Zaideé
Zaimara
Zaimarys
Zair
Zaira
Zairimar
Zaismely
Zamailly

Zamarie
Zamary
Zarahy
Zareima
Zarelis
Zarely
Zaria
Zaritma
Zasha
Zaskia
Zayara
Zayda
Zaymara
Zayra
Zcheika
Zeisha
Zekarish
Zeleyca
Zelibeth
Zelma
Zenaida
Zenayda
Zenia
Zennia
Zereida
Zeyhashlee
Zeymarie
Zilkia
Zilma

Zilmarie	Zoribel	Zulgey
Zindy	Zorimar	Zulianie
Zinia	Zoritza	Zulie
Ziomary	Zory	Zulimar
Zoa	Zorybeth	Zulimi
Zobeida	Zoryleen	Zulin
Zobeyda	Zorylis	Zulinet
Zohamie	Zorymar	Zulivette
Zohemy	Zoybet	Zully
Zohima	Zuania	Zulma
Zoidariam	Zuheidi	Zulmara
Zoila	Zuheila	Zulmari
Zolimar	Zuheill	Zulmaria
Zolis	Zuheiri	Zulmarie
Zollianne	Zuheyli	Zulmary
Zomary	Zulaika	Zulymar
Zoogey	Zulaydi	Zumara
Zor	Zulei	Zunilda
Zoraida	Zuleida	Zurelis
Zoraidaliz	Zuleika	Zurisadai
Zoraigelyn	Zuleima	Zuritza
Zoraimee	Zuleine	Zusette
Zorangelie	Zulema	Zwinda
Zoraya	Zuleyca	Zylkia
Zorayda	Zuleyka	
Zorelee	Zuleyma	

BABY NAMES FOR BOYS

BABY NAMES FOR BOYS

A

Aarón
Abber
Abdel
Abdías
Abdiel
Abdon
Abel
Abiazail
Abiezer
Abimael
Abimanuel
Abimelec
Abnel Joel
Abner
Abnol
Abrahim
Absalon
Aburie

Acisclo
Adalberto
Adelino
Adenis
Adiel
Adman
Adnel
Adriel
Agapito
Agripino
Aguedo
Ahmed
Alcides
Aldred
Alejo
Alexi
Alicesar
Alnardo
Alvinjoel
Amadis

Amalio
Ambrosio
Amek
Amhid
Amid
Amil
Amilcar
Amin
Amircal
Amisael
Amyr
Anardy
Anastacio
Ander Amil
Aneudy
Angel David
Angel Yamil
Angelino
Aniceto
Aniel

Anstrong
Antolino
Aquilino
Aranis
Arcadio
Argenis
Arístides
Armides Josué
Artemio
Ashael
Asterio
Atanacio
Audas
Audberto
Auddy
Aureo
Auro
Ausberto
Avelino
Awildo
Axel Yamil

B

Balbino
Baltazas
Bartolo
Baudilio

Belarminio
Bengie
Benigno
Benito
Benjacob
Benny
Benyamil
Berman
Bernardino
Berney
Bladimir
Blas
Blasino
Bonacio
Bonifacio
Bonosio
Boris
Brando
Brayan
Brayans
Bryan Amaury

C

Caleb Adiel
Calixto
Candelario
Carlos Yamil

Carmelo
Carpio
Carvajal
Casildo
Casimiro
Catalino
Cayetano
Ceasar
Ceferino
Celestino
Cesareo
Chariel
Chasidy
Chean
Chemán
Chinwandul
Christeve
Christian Obed
Cipriano
Cirito
Clodomiro
Confesor
Crispín

D

Damaso
Dariel

Darwin
Dativo
Daxel
Delfín
Demencio
Demetrio
Denzel
Deonicio
Dereck
Derek Jarek
Deric
Derick
Derik
Dido
Dillian
Dimas
Dionisio
Diosis

E

Ebel
Ebenezer
Edelmiro
Ediberto
Edil
Edilberto
Edmanuel

Edmundo
Edwardo
Edwell
Eladi
Eladio
Elbert
Eldel
Elenio
Eleuterio
Eliad
Eliamil
Elidio
Eliel
Elier
Eliezel
Eliezer
Eligio
Elimael
Elio
Eliodoro
Elisamuel
Eliser
Eliú
Eliud
Eliut
Elliam
Ellis Joel
Elliut
Elmo

Elnardo
Eloino
Elpidio
Elso
Eluis
Eluterio
Elvin
Elvin Jetziel
Elvins
Elycar
Emérito
Emigdio
Emil
Emill
Emmanuel Lou-
briel
Endel
Enoc
Enoth
Enriquillo
Enudio
Epifanio
Erasmo
Erasto
Erdy
Erik
Erison
Ermelindo
Ermenegildo

Ervin
Esaud
Esmeraldo
Estaquio
Estebany
Etanislao
Etervino
Etiel
Eugenio
Eulalio
Eulices
Eulises
Eulogio
Eurico
Eusebio
Eustaquio
Eutimio
Evangelio
Evangelito
Evaristo
Evaristo Eddie
Evelio
Evelío
Ezequiel
Ezra

F

Falmar
Faustino
Feliberty
Felíz Antonio
Fernan
Florencio
Florentino
Fortunato
Fractuoso
Francis
Frankel
Frankie
Franklin
Freddie Yamel
Fredesvi
Frewi
Frilly Josue Joel
Froilan
Fructuoso
Fundador

G

Gabino
Gaddiel
Gadiel

Gamaliel
Gamalier
Genaro
Geodanny
Georgie
Geovanni
Geovannie
Geovanny
Geovenny
Geraldo
Gered
Germane
Gervasio
Gian
Gian Carlo
Gian Kevin
Giancarlo
Gidel
Gieron
Gildo
Giovanell
Giovaniel
Giovanny
Gladimil
Godofredo
Graciliano
Gualberto
Gualdemar
Guillermok

Gumercindo
Gumersindo

H

Hainze
Hajime
Harito
Heber
Hector Yamil
Heliodoro
Heraclides
Heranfel
Heri
Hermenegildo
Hermenegindo
Hermer
Hermes
Hervert
Higinio
Hilario
Hipólito
Hiro
Hubert

I

Ian Yaxiel

Ibrahims
Idaleccio
Idamith
Idefonso
Ildefonso
Irvin
Irving Jose
Isac
Isair
Isander
Isidoro
Ismer Javier
Issachar
Itzairo
Ivisnel

J

Jaddyer
Jadid
Jadiel
Jael
Jafet
Jagmel
Jairo
Jamal
Jamil
Jan

Jan Paul
Jancy
Jandani
Janiel
Jantzen Alexis
Japhet
Japhet Damian
Japheth
Jarek
Jarim
Jasiel Joel
Jatziel Omar
Jawy
Jaycob
Jayden
Jayson
Jean Carlos
Jeancarlos
Jeanmichael
Jeffry José
Jefred
Jehiel
Jenaro
Jeremmie
Jeremy Isac
Jeriel
Jester
Jesus Harold
Jetziel

Joatam
Jocabed
Joelo
Joemanuel
Joeza
Johnavye
Jomanny
Jomar
Jonathan Yoshy
Jonathaniel
Jonie
Jordan
Jordanny
Jordany
Jose Antoni
Jose Johnavye
Joseamid
Josean
Joselo
Joshuabel
Joshuael Alexander
Joshuam
Josiel
Jossan
Jossy
Josuan
Josue
Josymael
Jouhan

Jouhna
Jouseph
Jova
Jovan
Jovany
Jowel
Juan De Dios
Juan Yomar
Junisther
Juvencio

K

Kahlil
Kelvin
Kelvin Yahdiel
Kendry
Keniel
Kenn
Kennen
Kenny
Kermit
Keven
Keyvan
Kidanny
Kriss

L

Lando
Lao
Leandro
Leberato
Leiram
Lemuel
Lener
Lenny
Leocadio
Leomar
Leoncio
Leopoldo
Leovardo
Leovigildo
Leslie
Lesther
Lexter
Liborio
Lino
Lionel
Lionel Alexis
Lisandro
Lizander
Lizardo
Longino
Lope
Loyda

Lucio
Luigadiel
Luis Amadis
Luis Yeniel
Lupercio
Luz Celenia
Lydio
Lyndon

M

Magdaleno
Manlio
Manolin
Marcelino
Margaro
Mariano
Massy
Mawil
Maximino
Maysonet
Medardo
Melvin
Melvis
Melwin
Merquiádez
Mervin
Michael Lee

Micheal
Milton
Misael
Mitchel
Modesto
Monse
Mortimer

N

Nadir
Naldo
Narciso
Natanael
Natanel
Nathanael Josué
Neftalí
Neftaly
Neftarl
Nefty
Nehemías
Neldy
Nemecio
Neville
Nicanor
Nicasio
Niconor

O

Obbed
Obed
Obrian
Odilio Albert
Olimpio
Omile
Onesto
Onix
Opildo
Orlan
Ortelio
Otilio
Otoniel
Oveth
Owen

P

Papías
Paulino
Pelayo
Pelegrin
Perfecto
Plinio
Policarpio
Porfirio
Presbitero

Primitivo
Prisco
Prudencio

Q

Quintín

R

Ragíl
Raimundo
Ralphie Reuben
Ramil
Ramses
Randier
Raniel
Raymundo
Regalado
Reinald
Reinerio
Remigio
Renato
Restituto
Reubén
Reyn
Rigoberto

Roddy
Rodney
Rodo
Romer
Romualdo
Rómulo
Ronaldo
Rosendo
Ruperto

S

Sabino
Sadiel
Salustiano
Sanjurjo
Santos Eulogio
Saturnino
Saturnio
Seferino
Seifert
Severiano
Shalom
Shorty
Sigfred
Sigfredo
Sigfrido
Silbestre

Silvestre
Sinesio
Sirio
Sixto
Solivan
Stalin
Susano

T

Tedwin
Telésforo
Tenislao
Teófilo
Tereso
Tiburcio
Tito
Tomy

U

Ubaldino
Ulpiano
Ulsino
Urayoán
Urbano
Uriel

V

Vince

W

Wady Enrique
Wael
Waldemar
Wallace
Wascar
Washington
Wellington
Welmer
Wenceslao
Wendel
Wendeleez
Wendell
Wendoline
Wenseslao
Wenther
Wesley
Widenzon
Wigberto
Wilberto
Wilfred
Wilfredo
Wilhem

Wilkins
Will Xavier
Willnel
Wilmer
Wiriel
Wiso

X

Xandel

Y

Yacoub
Yadian Joel
Yadiel
Yadiel Joel
Yadiell
Yadriel
Yael
Yafet
Yaffet
Yahdiel
Yahir
Yamil
Yamil Doel
Yamill

Yamilo
Yamir
Yandel
Yandiel
Yanel
Yaniel
Yariel
Yasser
Yazan
Yeison
Yeniel
Yeriel
Yomar
Yomil
Yoniel Adnel
Yoshy

Z

Zabdiel
Zenon
Zoher
Zoilo
Zuriel

NAME COMBINATIONS
FOR GIRLS

COMBINATIONS WITH
"LIZ", "LIS", "LYS" & "LEE"

Abiliz	Anellys	Brendalee
Adalis	Angelee	Brendalis
Adaliz	Angeliz	Brendaliz
Adarelys	Angelys	Brendalys
Adelis	Angiliz	Brialis
Adializ	Annjoslys	Brildalis
Agracelis	Anyelys	Carelis
Aidalis	Aranyelis	Carelys
Aideliz	Aremelis	Celis
Airaliz	Aricelis	Charilys
Alys	Artdalis	Cheryliz
Amarelis	Arylis	Chrisdaliz
Amareliz	Audeliz	Daibelis
Amarelys	Aurelis	Dalis
Amerilys	Auronelis	Damalis
Amirelis	Ayvialis	Damarilys
Anacelis	Bebalis	Damirelys
Analiz	Beisaliz	Danaliz
Andrealiz	Benalis	Danelis

Danelys
Danielys
Darelis
Darielys
Daybelis
Delis
Diadeliz
Dialis
Dianeliz
Doraliz
Doriliz
Eislee
Elis
Eliz
Ellis
Emelee
Emilys
Enadilis
Evaliz
Evelis
Eveliz
Florangelis
Flordeliz
Francheliz
Franshelis
Fransualis
Gabrieliz
Giselys
Gisselys

Glaricelis
Glendalis
Glendaliz
Glendalys
Glewyndaliz
Glorieliz
Glorylee
Gricelis
Grisdeliz
Grysseyliz
Hecdalis
Hecmarelis
Hectlys
Hiramilis
Horialis
Iberelis
Idalis
Idaliz
Idalys
Ideliz
Idualys
Ileangelis
Inelis
Iralys
Ireliz
Irelys
Iriselis
Irmalis
Irmarilis

Ivelis
Ivelys
Izomalee
Janelee
Janeliz
Janellys
Janelys
Janiellys
Janielys
Janiraliz
Jarelis
Jarielys
Jaychaliz
Jeannelis
Jelis
Jeniliz
Jenillee
Jennylee
Jennyliz
Jeyliz
Jisselys
Jogalys
Johalys
Josey Mirelys
Kareliz
Karellys
Karelys
Karielys
Karlaliz

Kaylaliz
Keidaliz
Keilee
Keimalys
Kelly Janellys
Kenia Lee
Kenuelys
Keyla Liz
Keylee
Kiara Lee
Kiara Lis
Kiaralis
Kiaraliz
Kichayra Lee
Kimberlys
Koralys
Laurelys
Leemagdali
Leexandra
Leeziy
Liannelys
Liceliz
Lidelys
Lisaira
Lisanaeli
Lisandy
Lisangela
Lisaura
Lisbelle

Lisela
Lisell
Liset
Lisnel
Lissuannette
Lixalis
Liz Yinellys
Liz Yinellys
Lizaida
Lizalee
Lizalee
Lizanne
Lizaries
Lizayra
Lizbel Cristina
Lizbenette
Lizceidy
Lizdalia
Lizdeika
Lizdianel
Lizeida
Lizelyn
Lizmaira
Lizmeliz
Liznei
Liznel
Liznelly
Liznelt
Llarilys

Lourdeliz
Luznatalee
Lynelis
Lysandra
Lysbeth
Lyset
Lyska
Lysmarie
Lysmaris
Lysset
Lyssette
Lyssie
Lysvette
Madalis
Magalis
Magalys
Magdalis
Magdelis
Magdilis
Maibelis
Maibeliz
Mairilys
Maradalis
Maralis
Maraliz
Maranyelis
Marelis
Mariadelys
Marianellis

Mariangelis
Mariangelys
Maridelis
Marieliz
Mariellys
Marielys
Marisoliz
Marlis
Marva Lee
Meralys
Mervaliz
Midelis
Mignaliz
Mindelys
Minelis
Mineliz
Miraidaliz
Mirelis
Mirelys
Mirnaliz
Mydalis
Myralis
Myreliz
Myrnaliz
Myrnelis
Nachaliz
Nadyalee
Naelis
Nahirlee

Naikalee
Nardaliz
Naycha Liz
Nayelis
Nayeliz
Naylis
Nayrimlee
Neimylis
Nelis
Nellys
Nildalis
Nilis
Nitzaliz
Nixsaliz
Noelis
Noralee
Noralis
Noraliz
Noreliz
Norelys
Normaliz
Olgalys
Omarilys
Onellis
Orialis
Orializ
Osilys
Raxelis
Reinalis

Reinaliz
Rosalis
Rosaliz
Rutdaliz
Saaelis
Sadoyeliz
Sairelis
Samaeliz
Sarangelys
Sashalee
Soangelis
Soralis
Sorializ
Sorieliz
Suhalee
Sulis
Surelys
Tairaliz
Vildaliz
Vinelis
Wandalis
Wandalys
Wendalee
Wendeliz
Wendilee
Wendilys
Wendylis
Widalis
Widalys

Wildalis
Wildaliz
Wildalys
Wildelis
Wildelys
Willmeliz
Wilmelys
Xionelys
Yaidilee
Yairelis
Yalis
Yamalis
Yamalys
Yamaralys
Yamilis

Yandeliz
Yanelis
Yanilee
Yaniralys
Yaraliz
Yarelis
Yareliz
Yarellys
Yarelys
Yarielis
Yarilis
Yarilys
Yaselis
Yasilis
Yasmarieliz

Yeiliz
Yinellys
Yiralee
Yminelis
Yodallys
Yoliz
Yonaidaliz
Zarelis
Zeyhashlee
Zolis
Zoraidaliz
Zorelee
Zorylis
Zurelis

COMBINATIONS WITH
"ANN", "ANNETTE" & "ANE"

Adriannette

Alexlyane

Aneida

Anel

Anelisa

Anellys

Aneris

Aneshka

Annelisse

Anneris

Annexaida

Annick

Annielith

Annjoslys

Annyoly

Cesiannette

Dannette

Dayane

Deliann

Doriann

Eliann

Eliannette

Gelliann

Gladyann

Gloryann

Illiane

Ivannette

Jashai Annette

Jeannette

Jeniann

Joann

Joannette

Kariann

Leshliane

Lissuannette

Loriann

Luzuannette

Merylane

Milliane

Oriann

Rosemarieann

Shelyann

Soane

Suannette

Valiann

Windyannette

Yolane

Yuliane

Yuriann

COMBINATIONS WITH "ITZA" & "IXA"

Aitza	Itzaira	Leixa
Aixa	Itzamar	Maritza
Angelitza	Itzary	Melitza
Anitza	Ixa	Militza
Anixa	Ixaivia	Mititza
Belitza	Jaitza	Mylitza
Charitza	Janeixa	Naitza
Claraitza	Janitza	Neditza
Dalitza	Jaritza	Neitza
Daritza	Jelitza	Nelitza
Denitza	Jenitza	Neritza
Doritza	Jeritza	Nixa
Eitza	Jhaitza	Ritza
Evelitza	Jhanitza	Samitza
Gitza	Jinitza	Saritza
Gloritza	Julitza	Shalitza
Idette Yarixa	Junitza	Shera Yaitza
Itza	Karitza	Thais Yaitza
Itzahyana	Kelitza	Violitza

Xenia Aixa   Yamitza   Yeitza
Yaditza   Yamixa   Yelitza
Yadixa   Yaniritza   Yenitza
Yahitza   Yanitza   Zoritza
Yaitza   Yarilitza   Zuritza
Yaixa   Yaritza
Yalitza   Yarixa

COMBINATIONS WITH
"MARIE", "MARY", "MARIS" & "MERY"

Abellemarie

Adelmarie

Ademaris

Adimarie

Agmarie

Aidimarie

Alimaris

Allymaris

Almarie

Bethmarie

Betzmarie

Carimarie

Carlysmary

Celesmarie

Chrismarie

Clarymarie

Dacmaris

Dagmarie

Dagmaris

Dagmary

Dalmarie

Damarie

Damary

Daumarie

Desmarie

Deximary

Diamaris

Didmarie

Dimarie

Dimaris

Dimary

Diomaris

Dycmarie

Dymarie

Dymaris

Edmarie

Edmary

Elimarie

Elismarie

Elymarie

Emmarie

Gamary

Germarie

Germaris

Gezette Marie

Gilmarie

Giomarie

Giomary

Gisellemarie

Glenn Marie

Gloriamary

Gretmarie

Greycha Marie

Grismarie

Guelmarie

Guimary

Gurian Marie

Hecmarie
Hecmary
Heisha Marie
Hermarie
Hildamaris
Ibelimary
Idamaris
Igmarie
Inmarie
Irmarie
Irmaris
Isamarie
Isamary
Ismarie
Ismary
Ivismarie
Jackmary
Jaimarie
Jamaris
Jashira Marie
Jaymarie
Jeanmarie
Jesamary
Jesmarie
Jesmary
Jessmarie
Jipsy Marie
Joanmarie
Joeny Marie

Johanny Marie
Jomarie
Jomary
Jormarie
Jossmarie
Joyce Marie
Jusmary
Karmarie
Katia Marie
Katilia Marie
Keishmary
Keymarie
Kiara Marie
Kiomarie
Kiomary
Kiomery
Lamaris
Leomaris
Lilmarie
Lumaris
Lumary
Lyanis Marie
Lychmarie
Lydimarie
Lymarie
Lymaris
Lymary
Lysmarie
Lysmaris

Marie Zulma
Marielix
Marieliz
Mariellys
Marielmi
Mariely
Marielys
Mariesely
Marisa
Marisel
Mariselix
Mariset
Marisoliz
Marissa
Mary Cheila
Marybet
Maryland
Maryliam
Marylisabet
Marytte
Melmary
Meryanne
Merylane
Meryssa
Milmary
Mimary
Mylmarie
Naymarie
Nechel Marie

Nelmary
Nemaris
Nermary
Nesmarie
Nicholle Marie
Nigmary
Nilmarie
Nilmaris
Nilmary
Nirmaris
Nismarie
Noemaris
Normarie
Normaris
Normary
Odemarie
Odemaris
Omaris
Rianchell Marie
Romaris
Rossmarie
Sachamarie
Sandimary
Selmarie
Shamary
Sharmarie
Sheylamarie
Silmarie
Silmary

Sofismarie
Solmarie
Solmary
Solymarie
Somarie
Sonmarie
Sulmary
Swimary
Sylmarie
Sylviamarie
Taismary
Tamarie
Taymarie
Taymary
Valmary
Velmaris
Velmary
Veramary
Vilkmarie
Vitmarie
Wilmarie
Wilmaris
Wilmary
Wilmery
Wylmary
Xaymarie
Xiomarie
Xiomary
Yamarie

Yamaris
Yamary
Yamirmarie
Yari Marie
Yazmarie
Yazmary
Yeechmarie
Yehimarie
Yeismary
Yelmaris
Yesmarie
Yolimarie
Yomarie
Yomaris
Yomary
Yormaris
Yosmary
Yulmarie
Yumary
Zamarie
Zamary
Zeymarie
Zilmarie
Ziomary
Zomary
Zulmarie
Zulmary

NAME VARIATION EXAMPLES
FOR BOYS & GIRLS

NAME VARIATION EXAMPLES
FOR BOYS & GIRLS

ORIGINAL	VARIATIONS		
Adolfo	Adolfina		
Adrián	Adriana		
Agustín	Agustina		
Alejandrino	Alejandrina		
Alejandro	Alejandra		
Alexander	Alexandra		
Alfonso	Alfonsina		
Andrés	Andrea		
Ángel	Ángela	Angelina	Angelita
Antonio	Antonia		
Arcadio	Arcadia		
Avelino	Avelina		
Basilio	Basilia		
Benito	Benita		
Cándido	Cándida		
Carlos	Carla		
Carmen	Carmelo		
Cecilia	Cecilio		
Claudio	Cluadia	Claudina	
Clemente	Clementina		
Cristina	Cristino		
Cristóbal	Cristobalina		
Daniel	Daniela		
Disonisio	Dionisia		
Domingo	Dominga		
Emanuel	Emanuela		
Emérito	Emérita		

ORIGINAL	VARIATIONS	
Emilio	Emilia	
Eric	Erica	
Ernesto	Ernestina	
Eugenio	Eugenia	
Fabián	Fabiana	
Fausto	Fausta	Faustina
Federico	Federica	
Fernando	Fernanda	
Francisco	Francisca	
Gabriel	Gabriela	
Giovanni	Giovana	
Gregorio	Gregoria	
Guillermo	Guillermina	
Herminio	Herminia	
Hipólito	Hipólita	
Inocencio	Inocencia	
Jacinto	Jacinta	
Jesús	Jesusa	
Joaquín	Joaquina	
José	Josefa	Josefina
Juan	Juana	Juanita
Julián	Juliana	
Julio	Julia	Juliana
Leonardo	Leonarda	
Lisandra	Lisandro	
Lorenzo	Lorenza	
Luis	Luisa	
Manuel	Manuela	
Marcelo	Marcela	

ORIGINAL	VARIATIONS	
Marcelino	Marcelina	
Margarita	Margarito	
María	Mario	Mariano
Máximo	Máxima	
Miguel	Miguela	Miguelina
Modesto	Modesta	
Nicolás	Nicolasa	Nicol
Octavio	Octavia	
Odilio	Odilia	
Patricio	Patricia	
Rafael	Rafaela	Rafaelina
Ramón	Ramona	Ramonita
Ricardo	Ricarda	
Roberto	Roberta	
Rogelio	Rogelia	
Rubén	Rubencia	
Salvador	Salvadora	
Sandra	Sandro	
Seferino	Seferina	
Simón	Simona	
Sixto	Sixta	
Teófilo	Teófila	
Teresa	Tereso	
Tomás	Tomasa	Tomasita
Valentín	Valentina	
Víctor	Victoria	

TOP 10 POPULAR NAMES
2006 - 2010

PUERTO RICO'S TOP 10 POPULAR NAMES FOR BOYS AND GIRLS 2006 - 2010

Every year, the Social Security Administration publishes the list of the Top 100 popular baby names per State, including Puerto Rico. The Popular Names section of the Social Security Administration website has a lot of features that you can explore. You can see name combinations for twins, how popular was your own name through the years, and the Top 5 names over the last 100 years! Here is Puerto Rico's top 10 popular names for boys and girls from 2006 - 2010.

TOP 10 NAMES OF 2010

RANK	BOYS	GIRLS
1	Luis	Mía
2	Ángel	Kamila
3	Ian	Camila
4	Sebastián	Alondra
5	José	Valeria
6	Diego	Amanda
7	Adrián	Gabriela
8	Carlos	Andrea
9	Dylan	Adriana
10	Derek	Paola

Source: http://www.socialsecurity.gov/oact/babynames/territory/puertorico2010.html

TOP 10 NAMES OF 2009

RANK	BOYS	GIRLS
1	Luis	Alondra
2	Ángel	Mía
3	Adrián	Valeria
4	José	Kamila
5	Diego	Camila
6	Sebastán	Amanda
7	Carlos	Andrea
8	Ian	Gabriela
9	Gabriel	Adriana
10	Yadiel	Alanis

Source: http://www.socialsecurity.gov/oact/babynames/territory/puertorico2009.html

TOP 10 NAMES OF 2008

RANK	BOYS	GIRLS
1	Luis	Alondra
2	Ángel	Camila
3	Diego	Kamila
4	Sebastián	Paola
5	José	Gabriela
6	Carlos	Amanda
7	Adrién	Valeria
8	Yadiel	Adriana
9	Ian	Andrea
10	Gabriel	Mía

Source: http://www.socialsecurity.gov/oact/babynames/territory/puertorico2008.html

TOP 10 NAMES OF 2007

RANK	BOYS	GIRLS
1	Luis	Alondra
2	Ángel	Gabriela
3	Diego	Paola
4	José	Alanis
5	Sebastián	Adriana
6	Carlos	Andrea
7	Yadiel	Valeria
8	Adrián	Camila
9	Gabriel	Amanda
10	Ián	Mía

Source: http://www.socialsecurity.gov/oact/babynames/territory/puertorico2007.html

TOP 10 NAMES OF 2006

RANK	BOYS	GIRLS
1	Luis	Alondra
2	Diego	Paola
3	Ángel	Gabriela
4	José	Alanis
5	Carlos	Adriana
6	Sebastián	Valeria
7	Yadiel	Andrea
8	Adrián	Amanda
9	Gabriel	Mía
10	Kevin	Génesis

Source: http://www.socialsecurity.gov/oact/babynames/territory/puertorico2006.html

Jared Romey

Suffering a typical 9-5 existence, Jared's foray into lunch-hour Spanish shook up his mundane life. He quit his job, stopped by briefly to school, and then left his country... for 14 years. Early stumblings in real-world Spanish taught him that a cola isn't just a soft drink, bicho doesn't always mean a bug, and boludo may be heartfelt or middle-finger felt. Nine countries, three business start-ups, two bestsellers and a Puerto Rican wife later, he is still confounded by how many Spanish words exist for panties. His quest is to discover all those words. In between, he meanders the Earth, dabbles in languages, drinks wine and sells shampoo.

Diana Caballero

Studied Marketing and Communications in Puerto Rico. She is an active collaborator of Speaking Latino writing blogs about language differences in Puerto Rico. She also helped in the compilation of the bestseller *Speaking Boricua: A Guide to Puerto Rican Spanish*.

Any comments, corrections or inclusions should be sent to
info@SpeakingLatino.com.

SpeakingLatino

Other books from Jared Romey's Speaking Latino series

Speaking Boricua
A Practical Guide to
Puerto Rican Spanish

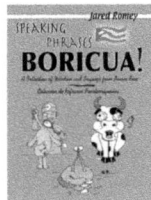

Speaking Phrases Boricua
A Collection of Wisdom and
Sayings from Puerto Rico

Speaking Argento
A Guide to Argentine Spanish

Speaking Chileno
A Guide to Chilean Slang

Follow Speaking Latino and Jared Romey

Facebook Pages
Speaking Latino
Jared Romey

Twitter
@jaredromey

Google +
Speaking Latino

Speaking Latino Website & Blog
Search the FREE database with more than 8,000 slang words and
phrases from Latin America at www.SpeakingLatino.com

www.ingramcontent.com/pod-product-compliance
Lightning Source LLC
Chambersburg PA
CBHW071624040426
42452CB00009B/1481